C000185367

IMAGES OF ENGLAND

WHITBY
THE SECOND SELECTION

Old Baxtergate in the 1880s. The street is a flattened 'S' in shape which followed the contour of the river when the street was first established around 1400. The street was built on a sandbank and was entirely residential until about 1700.

IMAGES OF ENGLAND

WHITBY
THE SECOND SELECTION

D.G. SYTHES

The bridge and east Whitby. John Tindale took this from the bucket of a crane, during the building of the Endeavour Wharf in the 1960s.

First published in 1999 by Tempus Publishing Limited
Reprinted 2001, 2005

Reprinted in 2011 by
The History Press
The Mill, Brimscombe Port,
Stroud, Gloucestershire, GL5 2QG
www.thehistorypress.co.uk

© The estate of D.G. Sythes, 2011

The right of D.G. Sythes to be identified as the Author
of this work has been asserted in accordance with the
Copyrights, Designs and Patents Act 1988.

All rights reserved. No part of this book may be reprinted
or reproduced or utilised in any form or by any electronic,
mechanical or other means, now known or hereafter invented,
including photocopying and recording, or in any information
storage or retrieval system, without the permission in writing
from the Publishers.

British Library Cataloguing in Publication Data.
A catalogue record for this book is available from the British Library.

ISBN 978 0 7524 1610 6

Typesetting and origination by Tempus Publishing Limited.
Printed in Great Britain.

Contents

Acknowledgements

I would like to express my appreciation for the encouragement, assistance and advice that I have received from Ernest Butler, without which I would not have started this book. Thanks must go to Bernard Nelson and Sidney Barnett, both Whitby-born and bred, themselves keen local historians, who have added items of interest which only those raised in Whitby could possibly know. Thanks also to the brothers Roger and Graham Pickles, joint Keepers of the Whitby Museum, with their Management Committee, for permission to publish the photographs in the collection. The royalties from this book, as with the last one, will go towards the preservation of the collection.

I thank the librarian, Mrs Durands and her staff for putting up with me being under their feet on numerous occasions, when my room would have been preferable to my company! Thanks once again to Bill and Mike Eglon Shaw, of the Sutcliffe Gallery, and to John Tindale for permission to use their photographs. Again posthumous thanks go to Hugh Lambert-Smith, Tom Watson of Lythe, the Doran family, and the many other long-gone photographers who gave their pictures to the museum as a record of their times, some of which I have used. Last, but by no means least, thanks to my wife Violet, whose love and support have made both books possible.

Introduction

The publication, *Around Whitby* of 1997 seemed to find a niche in the Whitby nostalgia market, and was well received by locals and visitors alike. Indeed it has been sent to ex-Whitby residents all over the world. It was at the request of local people, as well as the publishers, that a second selection was embarked upon. Well here it is. The book follows the same format as the previous edition, except that I have added extended chapters both on 'People' and 'Around The Villages', which I hope will find favour. The majority of the photographs have not been reproduced before, and those that have, have appeared infrequently.

In the two years since the last book was published there have been many alterations in the town. A huge cargo shed has been built on the Endeavour Wharf, though now that fewer ships use the port, many ask 'why?' The old post office building has been sold, gutted and rebuilt as a walk-through store from Baxtergate to New Quay Road. Additionally, on New Quay Road, one of Whitby's oldest surviving businesses, Collier's the ironmongers (in business since the middle of the nineteenth century), finally closed its doors, and with almost indecent haste was converted into a betting shop. As I write, New Quay Road has been closed, the port building on Endeavour Wharf demolished, and sheet piling has started in Dock End for a new sewerage scheme. When it has all been completed the centre of Whitby will be very different.

On the east side, the Seamen's Hospital has had its dwellings modernised, thankfully leaving the Gilbert Scott façade intact. Near Green Lane the old electricity generating site, itself the site of two seventeenth-century dry-docks, has been cleared and developed with housing which, in their sympathetic design, has at least given some thought to the area in which they have been built, and they blend in well.

Old Whitby, for good or bad, is being whittled away building by building, year by year. As you look at these photographs taken around a hundred years ago, and note the changes, you cannot help but wonder what the next century will bring, and wonder what chance Whitby, as we know it, has of surviving.

D.G. Sythes
Whitby, March 1999

The footpath leading to St Mary's, in 1890. Below the cliff, Henrietta Street is pictured with a miscellaneous range of temporary buildings. Most of what can be seen in the foreground has succumbed to cliff erosion in the present century.

Robin Hood's Bay

One

West Whitby

The top of Golden Lion Bank. No. 1 Flowergate was a butcher and game dealer, Ellen Berry. It is now the Sutcliffe Gallery. The doorway of the Unitarian chapel, built in 1715, still appears to house the same door today as the one that is pictured.

Downdinner Hill, seen from the site of the present Conservative Club, before Chubb Hill was cut through in 1886. The lowest house, mid-picture, is Arundel House; above that is Hanover Terrace. To the right are the fields where the County School was built in 1912 (Whitby Community College). The highest group of buildings are Upper Bauldbys and Mayfield Farm. To the left are Meadowfields House and, very indistinct, Airy Hill.

An immediate post-war aerial photograph, just above Whitby Grammar School (Whitby Community College). Below the school is the former sail loft and mill, now Beever's. Running from right to left is the former railway to West Cliff, and slightly above Prospect Hill is the roof of Meadowfields House.

Baxtergate, *c.* 1890. Falkingbridge's wine vault was the former chapel of ease that became redundant on the building of St Ninian's chapel in 1778. This old chapel was finally pulled down for road widening in 1925. The Temperance Hall was also demolished to make way for the London Joint Stock Bank, now the Midland Bank, in 1905. (Photographed by Frank Sutcliffe.)

A view of the little yard between the old chapel formerly known as Chalice House, and the Temperance Hall in Baxtergate, which was also swept away when the Temperance Hall was demolished.

Dock End, in the early 1930s. A new section of New Quay Road was built in the mid-1920s, and is shown here with the new piling prior to its completion in the 1930s. In front of the Railway Station the old Dock End is being filled in to its present-day proportions. The Angel Vaults in front of the Angel Hotel is the farthest of the two buildings on the Quayside; the other was the hotel garage. The Midland Bank, and St Hilda's Hall, are easily identified. The old building next to the bank is now the site of the small car park behind Mill's Café. In fact the only buildings in the foreground surviving today are the railway station, the Angel, St Hilda's Hall (Laughton's) and the bank.

Viewed in comparison with the above photograph is this one, also taken in the early 1930s. It shows Dock End from the site of the present-day roundabout. A noticeable feature is the street level in comparison to the present Dock End. Opposite is the 'Friendship' boathouse, moored off Tin Ghaut. This boathouse was built in the 1850s, and can still be seen up-river although in a poor condition.

Dock End car park in the late 1930s, prior to the construction of Endeavour Wharf and the building of the present New Quay Road. On the left Collier's still has its old shop frontage. Eve's Garage occupies the next two buildings in the present day. In the dock the dredger *Esk* lies alongside with St Michael's church behind. The car park is now largely taken up by a roundabout and taxi rank.

The lady in the pony and trap enjoys a joke with a friend at the end of Baxtergate. Falkingbridge's is now a betting shop, and above it until recently was HM Customs Office which closed in 1998, after more than 200 years of existence in the town.

Boots Corner. All the property is empty prior to its demolition in the early 1970s to allow for road widening after the reconstruction of New Quay Road. Note the cannon on the pavement outside Boots.

A parade passes down Wellington Road, in May 1910, having mustered at the railway station to proceed to the service at St John's church to coincide with the funeral of Edward VII in Westminster Abbey. A scene to remind us of a time when loyalty to the monarch was unquestioned.

The proclamation of the accession to the throne of George V, also in 1910. It would appear that there are as many people inside the station as out, looking through the right-hand station window.

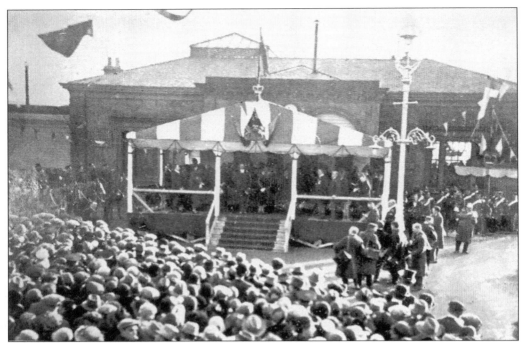

The Victory Parade after the First World War, in 1919. The civic stand and saluting base are outside the railway station while, in the photograph below, the troops parade on the site of the present bus station.

smiles, tears, of with the breath,
and, if God all my life!—
but love choose, I shall
death." thee better after

Casanova,

"I LOVE women," cries
Giovanni Vigliotto, the
middle - aged modern - day
Casanova who's been "mar-
ried" more than 100 times.
"They make me forget for a

The bottom of Flowergate in the 1920s. This block included Tindale's chemist and photographic business, prior to its removal to St Ann's Staith when this site was demolished to make way for Woolworths in 1929.

Scotch Head and the bottom of Khyber Pass, c. 1895. The Harbour Master's house is next to the Whitby No. 1 Lifeboat shed, at the foot of Khyber Pass. The Whitby No. 2 Lifeboat was housed a few doors down to the left, with the name board above the doors. Everything seen here has been swept away in the present century. In addition to the No. 1 and No. 2 Lifeboats housed along Pier Road, a third lifeboat was stationed at Upgang, just below the 'White House'. This boat could be launched on occasions when the Whitby lifeboats could not clear the harbour entrance. This pulling-lifeboat was instrumental in saving many lives from the frequent shipwrecks on the Sandsend beach during the nineteenth century, and also included service to the *Rohilla* in 1914. After the First World War, and the subsequent motorisation of the lifeboat fleet, the station was discontinued. Today there is nothing remaining except a short section of road which disappears over the cliff just above where this lifeboat house stood.

Lace stall. The market stalls were a familiar feature outside the harbour office at the foot of Khyber Pass during the summer months up to the outbreak of the Second World War, after which they were confined to the Market Square on the east side.

The Piers, coastguard lookout, and Argument's bathing machines were the subject of this Tom Watson photograph around the turn of the century.

The battery, from the West Pier, with the coastguard station. The battery embrasures were filled in with the pier alterations, but the powder houses remained, as they still do. It will be noticed that there are no railings along the piers. The capstan and mooring bollards were still being used for sailing and fishing boats, which were warped up the harbour if the wind and tidal conditions were wrong. The capstan bars can be seen under the seats.

Under the pier extensions in the 1950s. Then, as now, this was a popular place both for fishing and for those who just like to watch.

Whitby piers, at the end of the nineteenth century, with the magnificent globular gas lights. The lug-sailed fishing boats crossing the harbour bar are putting to sea watched by a group of visitors at the pier end.

Gibson's shop on St Ann's Staith. It will be noticed that the windows are placed sufficiently low for young noses to be pressed against them!

George Hooper's menswear emporium, also on St Ann's Staith. The business survived until the late 1970s. It is now a ladies hairdresser.

A Victorian photograph of the Royal Hotel, standing in almost splendid isolation on the West Cliff prior to the building of the Metropole in 1897.

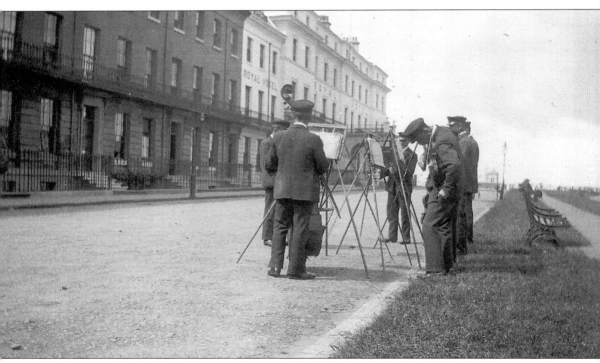

An itinerant band of musicians perform outside Kirby's and the Royal Hotels. There would appear to be a lack of an appreciative audience.

East Whitby from the west side in 1903. Part of the wall in the foreground is still extant, as are the entrance gate pillars. This was the entrance to Fishburn the shipbuilder's house, later to become a school. Today, to the left, is the police station.

The Whitby and District War Memorial Cottage Hospital.

The Whitby War Memorial Hospital, just after its opening by Princess Mary in 1925. The present Whitby Hospital occupies the same site.

The circus comes to town in 1904. This time the circus has probably arrived in town by train. The elephants are followed by a horse rider and camels, and are being driven past Broomfield Terrace on the way to their quarters, accompanied by the inevitable excited children.

A performing bear with its handler, who was said to be Italian, on Crescent Avenue at the turn of the century. Happily bears are no longer treated in this fashion in this country.

Walker's garage on Crescent Avenue in the 1920s. The site is now occupied by the Royal Mail sorting office.

Stakesby garage in the early 1930s, now Arundale's garage and showrooms. They sold National Benzol mixture petrol, as well as Singer, Morris and Hillman cars.

'Anyone for tennis?' These are the old tennis courts off Crescent Avenue, in the 1930s. The wall remains, though without the lettering. Within the wall is the car park, adjacent to the swimming pool, which today is situated on the courts where they are playing tennis.

Stakesby House in the 1880s with, presumably, members of the ship-owning Harrowing family admiring horse flesh. The house was later converted to self-contained flats, with additional buildings in the erstwhile grounds.

Meadowfields House, seen prior to its demolition. The present Meadowfields Estate was built in the grounds of this house.

Another Georgian house, which has been demolished and a small estate built on its grounds, is Field House, Upgang Lane. The only reminder of its former existence is the name – Field House Road.

This cottage stood in the former market garden which is now Pannett Park.

A North Eastern Railway locomotive, no. 1809, stands polished and gleaming opposite Esk Terrace.

Locomotives outside the Whitby loco shed, including a saddle-tank, no. 1763.

A Turnbull's steamer lies off the shipyard, c. 1905. It is seen from the Bog Hall signal cabin, just prior to the demolition of the Esk Inn (the buildings in the extreme right foreground).

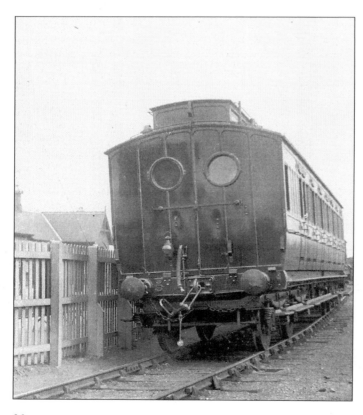

One for the railway carriage enthusiast – the first auto-car, at Whitby West Cliff in 1905.

An early 1930s charabanc outside Howard's garage, in Station Square. A trip to Scarborough, then to Thornton Dale returning via Goathland Moor, was 7s 6d. Next door to the garage (left) was Smithson's the plumbers. Between the Wellington Hotel and the garage (right) was the back entrance to the Clarence Hotel.

An omnibus stands in Station Square in the 1930s. In the background is the stationmaster's dwelling, a Georgian house that was purchased, with the land on which the station was to be built, in the 1830s. The site is now occupied by the telephone exchange.

New Quay Road, seen from the old bridge at the end of the nineteenth century. It shows the former chapel, standing alongside the bank and adjacent to Colliers. The narrow gap in between these buildings was the road into Baxtergate. The advertisements on the gable end of the mid-distant building include one for Freeman Hardy and Willis: 'Best Boots and Shoes'.

On the river side of the Boots corner building was this great spot for fishing, used by generations of small boys.

A fine study of the 1835 bridge at low water, by the Lythe photographer Tom Watson before the turn of the century.

Probably on the same day, the 1835 Whitby Bridge is pictured from the wooden quayside. This wooden structure was demolished on the building of the present bridge in the early years of this century. (Photographed by Tom Watson.)

Demolition of the piers of the old Whitby Bridge in 1907. In the background is the bottom of Golden Lion Bank.

The demise of W. Eglon's Neptune Fish Store, at the end of Haggersgate in the 1950s. A large block of property was demolished for road widening and redevelopment at this time.

WHITBY'S NEW BRIDGE.
pening Ceremony, July 24th, 1909.

Whitby's new bridge was opened on 24 July 1909. Among the opening party, to the left of the picture, is an elderly lady (to the right of the lady with the white coat). She was the guest of honour, having crossed the old 1835 bridge on its opening day seventy-four years earlier as a young girl. As can be seen, it was a great occasion in Whitby. The new bridge with its wider waterway would allow larger steel ships to be built at the Whitehall yard. It was, alas, seven years too late, for the emerging Hartlepools, with their nearby engine manufacturers could build ships much more cheaply. The Whitehall Yard closed for major shipbuilding in 1902.

Skinner Street in the 1930s prior to Horne's altering their shop front. The street has not changed greatly in the intervening sixty years; but the motor-car has made this sort of photograph an impossibility.

Flowergate near the junction with Cliff Street, in the 1920s. The nearside left house was the home of Stevenson the plumber.

Units of the German High Seas fleet bombarded parts of the east coast, from Hartlepool to Scarborough, including Whitby, in December 1914. Damage to a house on Spring Hill Terrace is pictured here.

The damage to a house on Windsor Terrace is seen after the bombardment of 1914.

An 1898 Temperance meeting at the end of the West Cliff, where the Marvic Nursing Home stands today. The newly built Metropole stands in isolation. In front of it stands the lookout, built by a retired mariner.

South Terrace at the top of Khyber Pass remains much the same today, with the exception of the railings which were cut down in 1940 as a sacrifice to the war effort.

Two

Whitby Harbour

The Sunderland-built, 242 ton brig, *Rachel Lottinga*, lies on the harbour bar in the late 1870s awaiting the tide. The ship was built in 1855 and was owned in Whitby from 1874. (Photographed by Frank Sutcliffe.)

In February 1955 the Army erected a Bailey Bridge across the harbour so that Whitby Bridge could be closed for repairs. The centre section was removable to allow river traffic access to the upper harbour. (Photographed by John Tindale.)

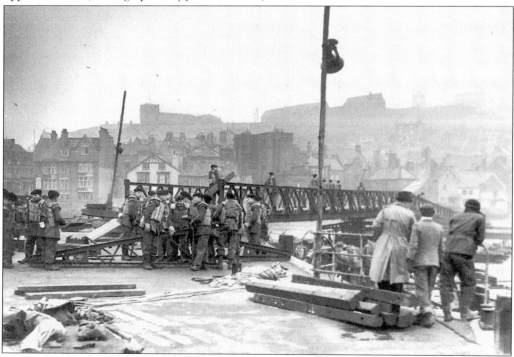

Two young lads with a wheelbarrow pause on New Quay Road in 1910. They stand among the boxes and empty barrels waiting to be filled with the catch from the tan-sailed fishing boats alongside.

Three youngsters pose in front of the big sailing-mules, c. 1910. Two of these were registered in Hull and Scarborough.

Dock End, in the 1870s. The old sailing vessel moored alongside the Angel Vaults is probably of 1830s vintage, or even older, with outboard chain-plates and an 'apple' bow. She would appear to be a hulk, probably for coal. Her topmasts and yards have been removed and her name painted out. The vessel on the right would appear to be in an equally bad condition, showing signs of having endured a very hard life. No sails are bent on the mizzen boom and part of her bulwarks are missing. It is probably early on a summer morning as there is not a soul in sight, which is unusual for Whitby! (Photograph by Frank Meadow Sutcliffe.)

The next five photographs are by Frank Meadow Sutcliffe. Dock End in its heyday at the end of the last century. Fish barrels are piled up awaiting shipment either by train, or by one of the sailing vessels moored opposite the Angel Vaults, which included a Cornish lugger among the mules and cobles.

On the other side of Dock End are the remains of the former shipyard site of Fishburn/Broderick. These rotting stumps were the site of the slipway which saw the last ship to be launched, some thirty years earlier, in 1862.

Seen from the opposite side of Dock End to the previous photograph, this again shows the old slipway with the former shipyard buildings. The site will be better remembered as occupied by Corner and Brown's timber sheds until recent years.

A Scottish 'fifie', poles her way towards the old Whitby Bridge in the 1880s. On the mud in the foreground are mussels ringed with stones, which were probably used for bait by the long liners.

In August 1872 the paddle-box of the steamer *Contest of Shields* caught under the beam of the pier side causing the vessel to heel over and sink on the rising tide. All the crew were saved, albeit with red faces.

Two boys watch a busy harbour scene with the herring boats alongside, *c.* 1890. For many years at high water, Dock End was prone to flooding. Later the harbour works and sheet piling cured the problem.

Some fifty years later pleasure craft dominate the scene, probably assembling for the annual Regatta in the late 1960s. (Photographed by Hugh Lambert-Smith.)

An assortment of craft, mainly Scottish Montrose-registered boats, are viewed from Marine Parade, c. 1910.

Foxglove lies off the Tin Ghaut slipway in the 1950s, in this atmospheric evening scene. (Photographed by Hugh Lambert-Smith.)

A view from Spion Kop in 1958. The Scottish herring fleet is moored along Pier Road. (Photographed by Hugh Lambert-Smith.)

One of the best remembered photographs by Hugh Lambert-Smith is this evocative shot of the herring fleet leaving Whitby for the night's fishing, with the afterglow of the setting sun on the sea and the mast and stern lights of the fishing boats receding into the distance.

These two photographs of 12 March 1906 show one of the highest tides ever recorded in Whitby during a storm. The height of this tide was not experienced again until 1953. Above, Tate Hill Pier and the Fish Pier are almost awash. Below, the bandstand and Pier Road are swept by a green sea running up the lifeboat slipway. Doubtless the absence of the pier extensions exacerbated the sea conditions inside the harbour. (Photographed by J.T. Ross.)

Forty-seven years later, the Doran Brothers photographed similar scenes during the great gale of 1953. Above, on Saturday 31 January, we see the high water which flooded much of the East Coast further south. Below we see the aftermath on Sunday 1 February. Two ladies struggle through the gale among the slabs of paving ripped up by the sea on the previous day.

FRENCH FISHING BOAT WRECKED
AT WHITBY, JULY 23RD. 1910.

A French fishing boat, *El Duc d'Aumale*, ran foul of the 'iron man' used in building the pier extensions on 23 July 1910. She had run on to the harbour bar initially, and was later (as seen below) washed ashore near the Spa Ladder.

The brig, *Star of Hope*, built in Whitby in 1854, came ashore in an easterly gale and snowstorm in December 1882. Her crew were taken off by the new lifeboat *Robert and Mary Ellis* on her first service. The ship was a total loss, remaining on the beach for several months. Part of her timbers washed into the harbour in March 1883.

The Russian barquentine, *Dimitry* (the nearer vessel), ashore outside the piers on the 25 May 1885. She was brought into the harbour, beached on Collier Hope, and there broken up. It was this ship that Bram Stoker, who was staying in Whitby at the time, featured in his fictional *Dracula* story.

The paddle tug *Nunthorpe* tows through Whitby bridge a new, Whitby-built, Turnbull steamer on the way to have her engine and boilers fitted on the Tees, in the 1880s. (Photographed by Frank Sutcliffe.)

The 1930s sailing coble, *Lily* WY 135, in the upper harbour. Skipper Bobby Allen steers with the seat of his pants, as he uses both hands to haul in the sheet.

Fishermen wait to unload the morning's catch from their cobles on a fine start to the day at New Quay in the early years of this century. In the background is the funnel of the steam yacht owned by Sir George Elliott, who financed the dredging of this part of the harbour.

The paddle steamer *Flying Fish*, of Bo'ness on the Firth of Forth, with the little schooner *Gem of the Ocean*, is moored on Church Street above St Michael's School, around 1907. All the warehouses on this side of Church Street were demolished fifty years later.

Turnbull steamers lie off the Whitehall Shipyard. They are, from left to right: *Darent*, built at Whitby in 1875, *Daisy* and *Pansy*, also built at Whitby during 1873.

A river fête, on 15 August 1890. All the boats are being towed through the open bridge, watched by a large number of people along Pier Road, Marine Parade and the bridge. This picture is reminiscent of the *Endeavour's* visit to Whitby in May 1997. (Photographed by Frank Sutcliffe.)

From Marine Parade, a variety of cobles and mules are seen in the early twentieth century, with a masting barge in the background. Its sheerlegs were used for stepping masts on the fishing boats. (Photographed by Doran.)

Three

East Whitby

The classic view of the east gable of Whitby Abbey (erected c. 1220), with its three tiers of triple Early English lancet windows. It was pictured from the abbey pond in the early 1950s. To the right against the boundary wall are three reconstructed windows from the choir. They were erected in the 1920s when the site was cleared of fallen masonry from the tower and nave. (Photographed by Hugh Lambert-Smith.)

A turn of the century view on Tate Hill Pier. A coble's sail is in the foreground. As every fisherman knows, there is always plenty of free advice from young and old when encountering a knotty problem.

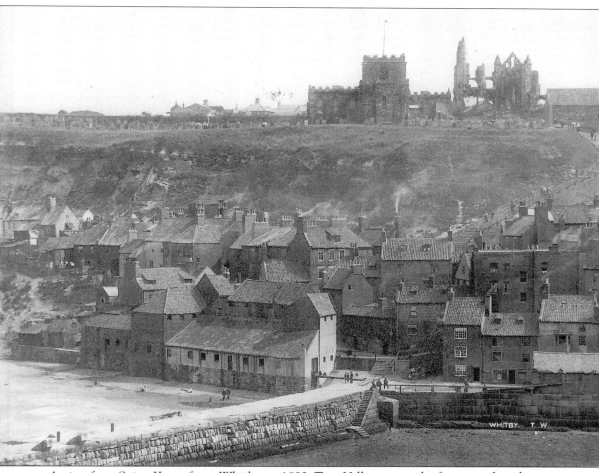

A view from Spion Kop, of east Whitby, in 1892. Tate Hill pier is in the foreground, with many of the buildings that have disappeared today. The large building on the sands, to the immediate left of Tate Hill Pier, was Sanders' sail-cloth factory, founded in 1756. It was in this building that the sails were made for Captain Cook's *Endeavour*, and for most of the whaling fleet. In the immediate foreground, on the pier, are the stone davits erected in 1822 for Whitby's first east side lifeboat. They survived until the 1970s, when they were cut off level with the pier – a crass piece of official vandalism. Most of the buildings on Tate Hill have been demolished to make way for post-war housing. In the background the 199 steps wind their way up to St Mary's church and the abbey. (Photographed by Tom Watson.)

The lifeboat house on Tate Hill Pier, which housed Whitby's east side lifeboat, is pictured in the late 1860s. It can also be seen from this that the buildings in Henrietta Street extended as far as the Spa ladder.

These fishing vessels were pictured at the fish pier, one misty morning in the late 1930s. (Photographed by Hugh Lambert-Smith.)

Above the harbour and just outside the walls of St Mary's, there was at one time a quarry. By the time of this photograph, in the 1880s, most of it had fallen into the sea, although a small building and some evidence of its existence remained.

When the buildings were pulled down at the end of Flowergate to build Woolworths, in 1928, this photograph was taken from the resulting gap.

A busy Church Street is seen from the top of Bridge Street, *c.* 1890. All the buildings on the immediate left hand side have been demolished. The buildings to the right have survived, and the building in the foreground is one of the oldest in Whitby, and still retains many of its fourteenth-century timber frames. Below it is the Society of Friends (Quaker) Meeting House. The original was built in 1676, and altered to its present form in 1813. Further down the gable end of Franklin's Coffee House can be seen, but all the buildings from here as far as Pickering's Wharf, with the exception of the 'Fleece', have now been demolished.

A.J. Bull's garage on Church Street, now the Endeavour garage. The petrol pumps were on the opposite side of the road, next to the warehouses which were demolished in the 1950s. To the right of the pump is Abraham's Bosom, which started here, ending where Pickering's Wharf now stands. It is hard to believe today that it was the only stretch of the river open to Church Street, and the place where, by tradition, the Penny Hedge was, and is, planted.

The top of the 199 steps and St Mary's churchyard in 1908. A visitor admires the Caedmon Cross, which had been erected some ten years previously, and a couple start the descent down to Church Street.

Bridge Street, looking towards Wilcox's Stores on Church Street, in 1954. The whole block was demolished in 1955. (Photographed by John Tindale.)

Looking down old Bridge Street from Church Street in 1954. All the buildings on the right, from the chemist's and including Cartridge's near the bridge, were demolished in 1956. (Photographed by John Tindale.)

Mrs Margaret Jane Smith stands outside her husband's public house the Greenland Fishery in 1899. This was one of the smaller pubs on Church Street.

The Old Market Place in the 1880s. Still recognisable today, and still used as a market. (Photographed by Frank Sutcliffe.)

The Wesleyan Methodist chapel on Church Street, built in 1762 and opened by John Wesley. It was pulled down in the late 1970s, and only the flight of stairs remains today.

Tin Ghaut from the river. Perhaps the most lamented of the east side buildings which were pulled down in April 1959. The site was made into a car park.

Mayor Harry Paylor proclaims the accession of Queen Elizabeth II on 6 February 1952.

A selection of horse-drawn carts off Church Street, on the site of the present Pickering's Wharf, at the turn of the century. In the background is the chimney of the electricity generating station at the foot of Green Lane.

Brewster Lane, which ran from Church Street
to the Fish Pier and formed part of the old
Shambles, is pictured in 1939. In the background
is the old Market Hall.

Seven Star Buildings, opposite the Market Hall,
in 1939.

Demolition of Green's Yard (at the top of Bridge Street/Church Street) in May 1955. The foundations of the former buildings in terraces show the density of housing.

Capella House in Ainstey's Court on the same site just prior to its demolition, also in 1955.

Four

Around The Villages

Whitby High Lights, between Whitby and Hawsker, in the late 1890s. The station was established and first lit on 1 October 1858. Of the two lights, the High Light is the lighthouse remaining, while the Low Light was dispensed with and pulled down in December 1890, being replaced by a fog-signal in 1905. The High Lights 57,000 c.p. light was visible for twenty miles, and was the last oil-burning lighthouse in England and Wales when it was discontinued in 1975 on electrification. The High Light was automated during 1991 and keepers were withdrawn in February 1992. The fog-signal, known as the Hawsker Bull, was finally silenced in January 1988, after which the property was put on the market and sold. Cliff erosion since the time of this photograph necessitated the public footpath outside the boundary wall, on which the boy is leaning, being diverted to the back of the lighthouse. (Photographed by Tom Watson).

The remains of one of Britain's first labour-intensive industries, alum mining and manufacture are seen in two views, *c.* 1880. The first shows the ravaged cliffs at Sandsend, which had been worked since 1607. Alum working had finished here by 1867, but the manufacture of Roman Cement, which had begun around 1811, was carried on until the end of the century. (Photographed by Frank Sutcliffe.)

Saltwick Nab was also a site for the mining and manufacture of alum from the local shale. It will be seen how much Saltwick Nab and the foreground cliff have diminished in the 100 years since this photograph. It is also hard to believe that there was a harbour of sorts in Saltwick Bay, but the post holes and stones are still extant, and a good imagination is all that is needed to put it all together.

Bloomswell, Robin Hood's Bay, in the 1890s. The water butts and the leather sea-boots would be the only things missing today from this almost unaltered scene. (Photographed by Frank Sutcliffe.)

Robin Hood's Bay near the bank top. This group of buildings still exists although they have been altered. The bank, however, remains unaltered and is just as steep. (Photographed by Frank Sutcliffe.)

An elderly gentleman pauses to looks into the beck at Robin Hood's Bay, in 1890.

At the bottom of Robin Hood's Bay in the 1930s.

A steam traction engine with a load of logs on Sandsend old bridge, which was washed away in 1910. In the background are the old cottages belonging to the alum works, which were behind them. These cottages were destroyed by a drifting sea-mine that exploded on the slipway during the Second World War.

An Edwardian lady and child on the beach on the Staithes side of Sandsend Ness. The cliffs show the ravaging scars of the alum workings. (Photographed by Tom Watson.)

This shows what a quaint spot old Sandsend was with its thatched squat cottages and horse-drawn traffic, in the 1880s. (Photographed by Frank Sutcliffe.)

Sandsend Beck, c. 1905. This is an area of Sandsend which has happily altered little in the intervening ninety-odd years. (Photographed by Tom Watson.)

Lythe Bank, on a windy day with a stormy sea running. In the background are the railway viaduct and the piers at Whitby without the extensions. This illustrates the hard life that horses led in hilly rural areas such as Whitby. (Photographed by Tom Watson.)

Modern farm equipment outside the old smithy at Lythe with Mr Dobson outside, around the 1920s or '30s. (Photographed by Tom Watson.)

Pictured outside the same smithy is William Ford, the local carrier, loading parcels for carriage, probably to the station.

Lythe Main Street featuring the local chapel, in 1902. (Photographed by Tom Watson.)

Children from the Roman Catholic School at Ugthorpe, *c.* 1905 pose for a picture. (Photographed by Tom Watson.)

Another group pose near Christ Church, Ugthorpe, probably on the same day.

Both of these pictures were taken on the Cowbar side of the beck in 1914. Above, an elderly lady wearing a Staithes bonnet walks down the harbour near the connecting bridge. Below, a fish auction takes place at the foot of the hill, with the large cod laid out on the bank. (Photographed by Mabel Oliver.)

Ruswarp village clusters around its church, *c.* 1910. The scene is viewed from Larpool Lane, which runs along the bottom of the picture.

The River Esk, from a little lane running off The Carrs at Ruswarp near the pleasure boat landing, *c.* 1910. The house in the foreground now stores the boats in the winter.

Sleights' old church, which was pulled down to make room for the present building. Many of these delightful Georgian churches were destroyed in the latter half of the nineteenth century during the Gothic revival. The church of St Nicholas, above Robin Hood's Bay, although unused, is of this period and has survived.

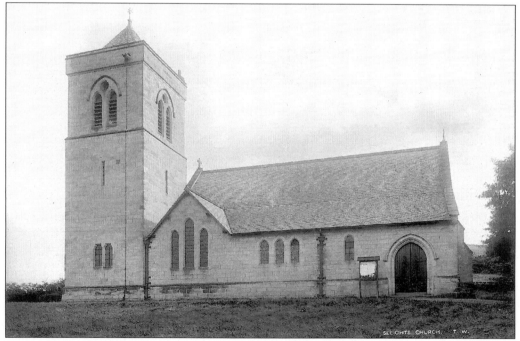

The replacement Sleights church, built further back from the road than the one above, is pictured in 1895. It was built in the Early English style, with triple lancet windows presumably intended to echo the gables of Whitby Abbey. (Photographed by Tom Watson.)

The road to Sleights Railway Station, with the Station Hotel – now named the Salmon Leap –
seen in the early 1920s.

Sleights village, from the side of Blue Bank in the 1930s. This shows the area prior to the later
development of this popular village.

Sleights' main street in the early 1900s. Above is a view looking down from Blue Bank. It is evidenced in many photographs of this period that Edwardians liked fresh air – all the windows being wide open. Today the road is the main route from Whitby to York and the A1. Many would wish that the traffic today was no busier than the solitary horse and cart pictured. Below, the tree-lined road with shop and houses leads up towards Blue Bank.

A family group pose at Westerdale, *c*. 1910. (Photographed by Tom Watson.)

Westerdale, probably on the same day as the above picture. To the left, it is interesting to note, there is what looks like a well-worn 'Monks' Trod'.

Hinderwell's main street with some of the locals outside their houses, *c.* 1910. The shop in the foreground belongs to G. Gibson, a butcher – probably the man standing outside. Further down is W.J. McClachlin's grocery shop. He also hired out ponies and traps, as well as closed carriages, according to the notice above his shop.

Castleton's main street, *c.* 1910. A group of children in mid-picture are outside an ice cream parlour, while further down the road a group of people gather outside what appears to be a saddler's business. The scenes here and above are very different today – parked cars now predominate.

The Black Bull at Ugthorpe, in the very early years of the twentieth century. Isaac Welford was the licensee. (Photographed by Tom Watson.)

Ugthorpe, early this century, with an Edwardian family at the gate. Further up the road at the gate of the next building, beyond the family, there is a clock mounted near the gate. Could it be that a clock-maker lived there?

An Edwardian view of Aislaby, outside what is now the village hall. Pond House is on the right, with the little group of terraced cottages to the left. It is a scene that happily remains much the same today.

Tom Watson moved his camera twenty-five yards and photographed this scene looking the other way from the one above.

Two views of Fylingthorpe village, looking towards Robin Hood's Bay, with St Stephen's church in the background. (Photographed by Tom Watson.)

When shown this 1911 photograph, many people could not believe this was Grosmont in its 'glory years'. The triple stacks of the blast furnaces stood where the picnic area and car parking are now situated for visitors to the North York Moors Railway. The platforms of the railway, with a locomotive, are in the foreground.

An elderly man poses outside the Station Hotel, at Grosmont, with its ecclesiastical ogee ground floor windows, c. 1907. In the background, men with a dejected-looking horse watch the proceedings.

Hinderwell Mill was built in 1828 seven storeys high. The mill was converted to steam around 1870, and the chimney and buildings for the machinery were erected about that date. The mill ceased working before the turn of the twentieth century and was allowed to fall into decay. It was finally demolished in 1955.

A cottage at Dale Head in Westerdale. Judging by the coronation border frieze of George V, on the wall paper right above the bunk, the year would have been around 1910. The appearance is of a bachelor's abode, maybe a shepherd, as a feminine touch does not appear anywhere. Many large families were raised in such humble surroundings, with the peat fire as the only cooking facility.

Five

People

A toddler on the west beach tackles the gritty problem of sand and ice cream, in the 1930s, by beginning in the middle and working outwards. (Photographed by Hugh Lambert-Smith.)

The Whitby boat-builder, Robert Gale, won the bronze medal at the 1851 Great Exhibition for his lifeboat design and model.

The Revd Francis Haydn Williams came to Whitby as Minister of the Unitarian chapel (built in 1715), which is still standing next to the Sutcliffe Gallery on Flowergate. He fell foul of the local clergy and landowners over footpaths and rights of way, particularly around the abbey. He was not averse to taking the law into his own hands, and once suffered the penalty of a short stay in prison for his pains.

An interesting group of railway workers,
in the goods yard shed at Whitby in 1888.
Included are the stationmaster and the
railway policeman (standing above him),
along with other worthies and workmen,
including the station dog which was probably
the rat catcher. (Photographed by Frank
Sutcliffe.)

The family of Mary Linskill, the Whitby
author. Mary is the lady standing on the right,
she died aged fifty in 1891.

Archbishop Thompson of York (centre) with the Revd George Austen, rector of Whitby (with stick) pose with members of the local clergy outside the Tin Tabernacle on the occasion of the laying of the foundation stone of St Hilda's on the West Cliff in 1883. The church was built on the same site and opened in 1885.

Last day at Greengates, the Chapman and Simpson Bank in Grape Lane, which was established in 1785. The bank closed in 1901 on amalgamation with the London Joint Stock Bank which in turn became part of the Midland Bank. The 'green gate' was reputed to have been preserved until recent years in the vault of one of the local banks.

The laundry staff of Mulgrave Castle, *c.* 1880.

'Flint Jack', of Sleights, was an accomplished flint knapper, and forger *par excellence*, who achieved notoriety by fooling most of the museums in the country, and indeed the world, with his 'prehistoric' flint axes and arrowheads.

John Richardson, the carrier, of Scarborough.

The next six photographs were taken by an American amateur photographer, John H. Tarbell, in 1889, and have never been published before. Frank Sutcliffe's fame was by this time becoming international through the exhibition work he was submitting to the various International Photographic Societies. Many of his admirers came to Whitby in order to meet him and to photograph the same subjects in the hope that some of the Sutcliffe talent would rub off. In this group of photographs Sutcliffe's influence is quite evident. In the first, a group of women and children are outside what are today the public conveniences, but in those days was Jonty Paylor's, in Station Square. The building behind, with the chimney, was the Railway Tavern, now replaced by the Tap and Spile, while across the road the railway station is easily recognisable.

At the foot of Tate Hill Pier, an adult presents her back to the camera, while a group of local children also studiously avoid looking at the camera.

A group of fishermen take a break to smoke a pipe along Pier Road.

In the same vein this photograph, titled 'Salting the Fish', won the silver medal at the American Amateur Photographers' competition at New York in 1890/91

Striking a rather heroic pose, this bearded fisherman sits on the thwart of his coble on the Pier Road sands. The inevitable small boy, cross-legged, with hands deep in his pockets, leans on the boat, quite unimpressed by the antics of 'grown ups'.

Arguments Yard, with some of the locals. It is a study of the poverty and conditions in which many of the Whitby fishermen lived with their families a century ago. Most of the buildings here have survived and have been modernised. It is a pity, with hindsight, that other yards such as Tin Ghaut did not.

Another American who came to Whitby in 1905, some fifteen years later than John H. Tarbett, was John Phillip Sousa who, with his famous band, played the marches that are as popular today as they were then.

Not as famous as John Phillip Sousa were Frank Gomez and the Municipal Orchestra, who played in Whitby for many of the pre-war years. He is pictured here in 1926 and is still fondly remembered by many of the older generation of Whitby.

The unveiling of the Captain Cook Memorial on the West Cliff, in October 1912. The money to meet the cost of the memorial was donated by local MP, Sir Gervase Beckett. The unveiling was performed by Lord Charles Beresford, who is seen here making a speech. The press table with its reporters is in the right foreground.

The Duchess of Albany opened the County School, later becoming the Grammar School, and even later Whitby Community College, on the 28 September 1912.

David Lloyd George, Prime Minister during the First World War, campaigns in Whitby during the 1931 elections. Seated next to him is Ramsey Muir. White Point is the house in the background

Speeches at the Spa for the Cottage Hospital Bazaar in 1925. Capt. Sydney Herbert is the speaker. Listening, from left to right are: Lady Harrowing, Miss Yeoman, Lady Marjorie Beckett, Lord Normanby, the Earl of Faversham, W.C. Headlam, Sir John Harrowing and E. Frankland.

Gray's shop on St Ann's Staith, a favourite shop for boys and girls. This group are with 'John the Bellman', the town crier who has his bell tucked under his arm. He was a favourite subject for Frank Sutcliffe and various artists, featuring in many photographs and paintings until his death in 1909.

A group with a water diviner work on the Mulgrave Estate during the 1890s. The men behind are carrying various tools, the other bearded man a handful of spare hazel twigs. It could be they were looking for a lost water pipe.

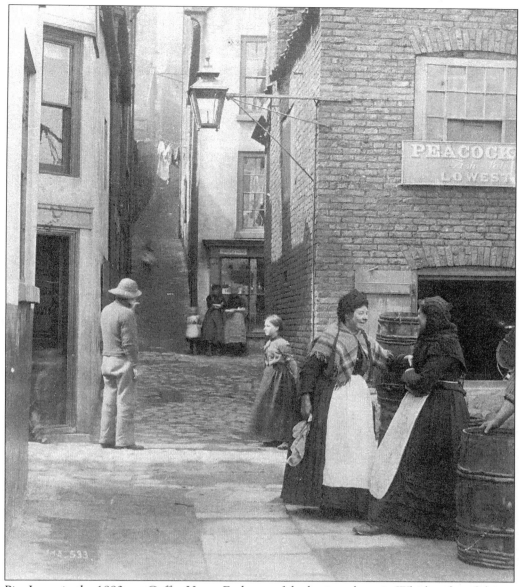

Pier Lane, in the 1880s, at Coffee House End, one of the busiest places in Whitby when fish was being sold. The site is not easily recognisable today except that the extreme left-hand wall, with only a window showing is the Marine Café – then it was the Marine Hotel. (Photographed by Frank Sutcliffe.)

Navy Day in 1908. HMS *Spartaite*, with other units of the Home Fleet moored off Whitby, was open to visitors. In the foreground a group of men learn the intricacies of the naval gun. In a few years many would get to know the subject only too well – from both ends. In the background, Jolly Jack eyes the ladies from the vantage point of the capstan.

A concert party on the west sands in 1905. The deck chairs cost 6d to hire and the show lasted about an hour.

Bridge End was always one of the popular meeting places of Whitby. In this Edwardian photograph there are plenty of loungers on the harbour rail having a 'crack'. In those days it was even safe to walk in the road!

Market day, on the cobbled Market Square outside the old town hall, on Whitby's east side in 1905. The little girl holding her brother's hand seems more interested in the photographer.

Frank Sutcliffe photographed John Ruskin, the art critic, in his garden, at the height of the critic's fame.

Meg Richardson, 'The Mussel Queen', working on the quay, in August 1932. (Photographed by Mr George, of Cinderford.)

A group of 1930s children enjoy a Punch and Judy show on the sands. Captured forever are the expressions of enjoyment, wonder, scepticism and disbelief on their faces. (Photographed by Hugh Lambert-Smith.)

A group of musicians of the Whitby String Orchestra, at the Eskdale Tournament of Song in 1951. (Photographed by John Tindale.)

Alan Major at the organ of the Empire Cinema in Whitby. This will jog many a memory.

Members of the Whitby Co-op in Sandgate during the 1930s. Among those pictured are: Phil Hoggarth (extreme left), Ted Parker (wearing apron) and Willy Tor (young man wearing apron).

Prize winners at Lythe School in 1950.

This picture could be in a competition to discover the collective noun for a group of eight nuns! They are seated near the Captain Cook memorial on the West Cliff sometime after the Second World War. (Photographed by Hugh Lambert-Smith.)

The next four photographs are portraits of former Whitby residents. Their lined faces demonstrate that their lives had involved hard struggle but all of them show the tremendous character that such a life bestowed on them. This is Mrs Hannah Smith, one of Whitby's characters in the inter-war years. She was known as 'Tricky' Ann because she declared that people tried to trick her on sales of the fish she traded from a basket in the town.

This elderly lady rests on a stone bench, and doodles with her walking stick outside her thatched cottage, in the late 1870s. (Photographed by Frank Sutcliffe.)

This old man, with a chin strap beard and a cast in one eye, is one of those, it can be surmised, who saw few of life's luxuries; many of which we take for granted today.

A lady who many would recognise as a typical grandmother from the first quarter of this century. Her bonnet would have reflected the area she came from. Like the fishermen's 'ganseys', each was made to be recognised as originating from a specific village.

A pipe-smoking gypsy sits outside her caravan, waiting for the kettle to boil in the 1930s. She sits on the Abbey Plain. (Photographed by Hugh Lambert-Smith.)

Hugh Lambert-Smith will be remembered in Whitby as an optician, with his business on Skinner Street. He established the business after service in the First World War as a pilot with the Royal Flying Corps. The optician's is now run by his successor John Hamilton Scott. Lambert-Smith liked nothing better than photographing ordinary people, doing ordinary things; like looking into shop windows, as in this picture.

This time it is children looking into a shop window at the 'goodies' on display. Many children in Whitby went barefoot, wearing their boots for school only.

The Brunswick Rooms attached to Brunswick church (seen in the following picture). The rooms are laid out for the tea that was provided to celebrate the opening of the rooms in 1891. (Photographed by Tom Watson.)

Whitby has always been proud of the number of pubs it supported in the nineteenth century. It could also be proud of the number of local preachers it supported. This group, on the steps of Brunswick Methodist church in May 1897, are Wesleyan. Add to these the numerous vicars and curates (seen on page 99), along with the Roman Catholic priesthood, the ministers and pastors of other denominations, and one realises that getting away with any 'sins' in Whitby would have been a matter of good luck rather than design.

'Fish Jane', a nineteenth-century version of 'Tricky' Ann. These fish-wives were a colourful part of the Whitby scene, and were painted and photographed by many aspiring artists and photographers. (Photographed by J. Stonehouse.)

One of the most prolific of our local historians came to the Whitby area in the early 1840s, as vicar of Danby – he was Canon J.C. Atkinson. This learned reverend gentleman, although seen here in the evening of his life, was not averse to learning to use the modern technology of the day, in this case the basket typewriter.

Combined operations. Coastguards and the Whitby Royal Volunteer Artillery are at drill at the battery on Whitby's West Pier in 1870. The cannon on the right is one of the old Napoleonic era muzzle-loading sixty-four pounders, which were kept in the harbour yard at the back of the harbour master's office.

Boys at Holgate's School at Princess House, on Spring Hill, Whitby, *c.* 1880. The house was known as 'Lobster Hall', and was built by the coachman of the York stagecoach who made enough money transporting lobsters to York to erect it. It eventually became a school. After a chequered career it was until recently the Princess Club. At the present time it is used as an annexe to Bagdale Old Hall.

A charabanc outing in the 1920s, organised by the Star Inn on Haggersgate. Among those pictured are: R. Eglon (the lifeboat coxswain), W.C. Brown, R. Walker, Tom Hoggarth, G. Dye, Matt Corner, J.S. Brown, W. Stamp, H. Stevenson. The driver is I. Tomlinson, and the coach belonged to Milburn's.

A group of Whitby ship-masters: Capt. Burnley, Capt. J.L. Cockcroft, Capt. Middleton, a captain of a Dutch steamship, and Capt. Storm.